A Doll's House

Henrik Ibsen

Abridged and adapted by Tony Napoli

Illustrated by Gershom Griffith

A PACEMAKER CLASSIC

GLOBE

Pearson

A Doll's House (Pacemaker)

Ibsen/Napoli
AR B.L.: 3.2
Points: 2.0   UG

Executive Editor: Joan Carrafiello
Project Editor: Karen Bernhaut
Editorial Assistant: Keisha Carter
Production Director: Penny Gibson
Print Buyer: Cheryl Johnson
Production Editor: Alan Dalgleish
Desktop Specialist: Margarita T. Linnartz
Art Direction: Joan Jacobus
Marketing Manager: Marge Curson
Cover and Interior Illustrations: Gershom Griffith
Cover Design: Margarita T. Linnartz

ISBN 0-835-91404-6
Printed in the United States of America

6 7 8 9 10   05 04

1-800-321-3106
www.pearsonlearning.com

Contents

Act 1 1
Scene 1 1
Scene 2 7
Scene 3. 15
Scene 4. 22
Scene 5. 30

Act 2 36
Scene 1. 36
Scene 2. 46
Scene 3. 53
Scene 4. 59

Act 3 65
Scene 1. 65
Scene 2. 73
Scene 3. 78

Cast of Characters

NORA HELMER	The main character of the play; a Norwegian housewife and mother of three children
TORVALD HELMER	Nora's husband; a lawyer who has just been made a bank manager
DR. RANK	A physician and close family friend of the Helmers
MRS. CHRISTINE LINDE	Nora's childhood friend
NILS KROGSTAD	A bank assistant and a moneylender
ANNE MARIE	The nursemaid for the Helmer children
HELENE	The Helmer family maid

ACT 1

The play takes place inside the home of Torvald Helmer and his wife Nora. The time is 1879, on Christmas Eve. The place is an unnamed city in Norway. Nora arrives home with Christmas presents and a tree. The couple discuss Torvald's promotion to bank manager.

Two visitors arrive. One is Dr. Rank, a physician and longtime friend of the Helmers'. The other is Christine Linde, Nora's childhood friend. Mrs. Linde tells Nora that she has come to town to find a job. Nora promises to see if Torvald can find her a position at the bank.

Nils Krogstad, a bank clerk, arrives. He asks Nora to talk Torvald into keeping him on at the bank. He threatens to reveal that she borrowed $1,200 from him by forging her father's signature. When Torvald returns, a desperate Nora tries to talk her husband into keeping Krogstad employed.

Scene 1

A pleasant room, with tasteful furniture. On the back wall, one door on the right leads to the entrance hall. A second door on the left leads to TORVALD HELMER's *study. The front door-bell rings.* NORA *comes into the room, humming happily to herself. She is carrying many packages. Behind her, a* PORTER *can be seen outside holding a Christmas tree and a basket. He hands them to the* MAID.

NORA: Hide the Christmas tree, Helene. The children must not see it before I've decorated it this evening. (*To the* PORTER) How much?

PORTER: Fifty öre.

NORA: Here's half a crown. Keep the rest.

(*The* PORTER *thanks her and leaves.* NORA *walks to her husband's study and listens at the door.*)

NORA: Yes, he's here.

(*She begins to hum again.*)

HELMER (*from his study*): Is that my little skylark singing out there?

NORA (*opening some of the packages*): It is!

HELMER: Is that my little squirrel frisking about?

NORA: Yes!

HELMER: When did my squirrel come home?

NORA: Just now. Come out here, Torvald. Come see what I've bought.

HELMER: You must not disturb me! (*Pause; then he opens his door and looks in.*) All that? Have you been overspending again?

NORA: Oh, Torvald. Surely we can let ourselves go a little this year! It's the first Christmas we don't have to scrape. You're making tons of money.

HELMER: My new salary doesn't begin until April.

NORA: So! We can always borrow until then.

HELMER: Nora! (*Walks to her and takes her playfully by the ear*) What a little spender you are!

Suppose I was to borrow a thousand crowns today, and you spent it all during Christmas. And then, on New Year's Eve, a tile fell off a roof and hit me on the head—

NORA (*with her hand over her mouth*): Don't say such horrible things.

HELMER: But suppose something like that did happen?

NORA: If something like that happened, I wouldn't care if I owed anyone anything.

HELMER: But what about the people I borrowed from?

NORA: Who cares about them? They are only strangers!

HELMER: Just like a woman! You know how I feel about these things. Never borrow!

NORA (*walking over to the stove*): Very well. Just as you say, Torvald.

HELMER (*following her*): There, there! My little songbird must not droop her wings, eh? (*Takes out his wallet*) Nora, what do you think I've got here?

NORA: Money!

HELMER: There! (*He hands her some.*) I know how these small expenses come up at Christmas.

NORA: Oh, thank you, Torvald. But come over here. I want to show you all the things I've bought—and so cheap! Look; here are some

new clothes for Ivar . . . and a little sword. There's a horse and trumpet for Bob, and a doll and cradle for Emmy. I've got some handkerchiefs for the maids.

HELMER: What's in this package?

NORA: No, Torvald! You must not see that until tonight!

HELMER: Very well. But tell me. What did my little spender want for herself?

NORA: For me? Well, I don't really know. But if you did want to give me something . . . you could always give me money. Only what you could spare. Then later I could buy something with it.

HELMER: But Nora—

NORA: Oh, please, Torvald, dear! I beg you. I'll wrap the money up in pretty gift paper and hang it on the Christmas tree. Wouldn't that be fun?

HELMER: What is the name of that pretty little bird that can never keep any money?

NORA: Yes, yes, squanderbird. But please let's do what I say. Then I'll have time to think about what I need most.

HELMER: If only you could keep the money I gave you. But you'll spend it on all kinds of useless things for the house. Then I'll have to dig into my pocket again.

NORA: Oh, but Torvald. . .

HELMER: You can't deny it, dear. (*Puts his arm around her waist*) My pretty little pet is very sweet. But what an expensive pet she is for a man to keep.

NORA: For shame! How can you say such a thing? I save every penny I can.

HELMER (*laughing*): You are a funny little creature. Just like your father used to be. Always on the lookout for money. But as soon as you have any, it just runs through your fingers. Well, I suppose I must take you as you are. It's in your blood. These things are hereditary, Nora.

NORA (*crossing to the table*): I would never dream of doing anything you didn't want me to. Did you remember to invite Dr. Rank?

HELMER: No. But he knows he'll be dining with us. Anyway, I'll ask him when he comes this morning. Nora, you can't imagine how I'm looking forward to this evening.

NORA: So am I. And how the children will love it. (*Takes his arm*) Now I've been thinking about how we might arrange things. As soon as Christmas is over. . . (*The doorbell rings in the hall.*) Oh, there's the doorbell. Someone's coming. What a bore.

MAID (*in the doorway*): There's a lady to see you, madam.

NORA: Show her in, please.

MAID (*to* HELMER): And the doctor's here too, sir. He's gone to your study.

Scene 2

The same room. HELMER *has gone into his study. The* MAID *shows in* MRS. LINDE, *who is in traveling clothes. The* MAID *exits.*

MRS. LINDE (*shyly and with hesitation*): Good evening, Nora.

NORA (*confused*): Good evening—

MRS. LINDE: I'm afraid you don't recognize me.

NORA: No, I'm afraid I—Yes, wait a minute— surely—Why Christine! Is it really you?

MRS. LINDE: Yes, it's me.

NORA: Christine! (*Gently*) How you've changed!

MRS. LINDE: Yes, I know. It's been nine years.

NORA: Has it been so long? Oh, these last nine years have been such a happy time for me! Now you've come up to town, too? That long journey in the winter! How brave of you.

MRS. LINDE: I just arrived this morning.

NORA: To enjoy yourself over Christmas, of course. Oh, how wonderful. We'll have such fun. Take off your things. You're not cold, are you? Now you look like your old self. But you are a little paler, Christine, and perhaps a bit thinner.

MRS. LINDE: And much, much older.

NORA: Yes, perhaps a little older. (*Stops suddenly and looks serious*) But how thoughtless of me to sit here and chatter away like this! Forgive me.

MRS. LINDE: What do you mean?

NORA (*quietly*): Poor, Christine. You've become a widow.

MRS. LINDE: Yes. Three years ago.

NORA: I know, I know. I read about it in the papers. Oh, Christine. I often thought of writing to you. But I always put it off. Something always came up.

MRS. LINDE: I understand, Nora dear.

NORA: No, it wasn't very nice of me. My poor darling, what you've gone through! He didn't leave you anything?

MRS. LINDE: No.

NORA: No children?

MRS. LINDE: No.

NORA: Nothing at all, then?

MRS. LINDE: Not even a feeling of loss or sorrow.

NORA (*looking at her in disbelief*): But, how is that possible?

MRS. LINDE (*smiling sadly*): Oh, these things happen.

NORA: How very sad that must be for you. I have three lovely children. And you heard about the wonderful luck we've had? My husband has just been named bank manager !

MRS. LINDE: Your husband! Oh, how lucky!

NORA: Isn't it? Being a lawyer is not a very steady way of making a living, you know.

From now on, we'll be able to live quite differently. We'll do just what we want.

MRS. LINDE: Yes. It must be nice to have enough to cover one's needs, anyway.

NORA: Not just our needs! We're going to have lots and lots of money!

MRS. LINDE (*smiling*): Nora, Nora. Haven't you grown up yet? When we were at school, you were a terrible little spender.

NORA: Torvald says I still am. (*Wags her finger*) But little Nora isn't as silly as everyone thinks. Oh, we've been in no position for me to waste money. We've both had to work.

MRS. LINDE: You, too?

NORA: Yes, odd jobs—sewing, embroidery, things like that. (*Casually*) Torvald left his job when we got married. He had no chance of advancement in his department. For the first year, he had to take on all sorts of extra jobs. He worked day and night. He became very ill. The doctors said he'd have to go to a warmer climate.

MRS. LINDE: You spent a whole year in Italy, didn't you?

NORA: Yes. We had to go. Oh, it was a marvelous trip. It saved Torvald's life, but it cost an awful lot of money.

MRS. LINDE: I can imagine.

NORA: Twelve hundred dollars.

MRS. LINDE: How lucky that you had it.

NORA: Well, actually we got it from my father.

MRS. LINDE: Oh, I see. Didn't he die about that time?

NORA: Yes, just about then.

MRS. LINDE: I'm sorry. I know you were very fond of him. But after that you left for Italy?

NORA: Yes. We had the money then, and the doctors said it was urgent.

MRS. LINDE: And your husband came back completely cured?

NORA: Fit as a fiddle!

MRS. LINDE: But I thought the maid said that the gentleman who arrived with me was a doctor.

NORA: Yes, that was Dr. Rank. But he doesn't come because anyone is ill. He's our best friend. He looks in on us at least once a day. (*Jumps up and claps her hands*) Here I am talking about nothing but myself. Oh, please don't be angry with me! Tell me, is it really true that you didn't love your husband? Why did you marry him, then?

MRS. LINDE: My mother was helpless and bedridden, and I had my two little brothers to take care of. I just couldn't say no.

NORA: I suppose you're right. I guess he was fairly wealthy, then?

MRS. LINDE: He was quite well off, I believe. But the business was shaky. When he died, it went bankrupt, and there wasn't anything left.

NORA: What did you do?

MRS. LINDE: Well, I had to try to make ends meet somehow. I started a shop and a small school. These last three years have been one long slog for me, without a minute's rest. But now it's over, Nora. My poor dear mother has passed away, and the boys don't need me anymore.

NORA: How relieved you must be.

MRS. LINDE: No. Just empty. I have nobody to live for anymore. (*Restlessly*) That's why I couldn't stand it there any longer, cut off from the world. I thought it would be easier to find some work here to occupy my mind. If only I could find a steady job—perhaps in an office.

NORA: Oh, I understand. You think maybe Torvald might be able to do something for you?

MRS. LINDE: Yes, I was thinking that.

NORA: He will, too. Just leave it to me. Oh, I do so want to help you.

MRS. LINDE: It is very sweet of you to bother so much about me. Especially since you know so little of the worries and hardships of life.

NORA (*tossing her head*): I wouldn't be too sure of that if I were you.

MRS. LINDE: Oh?

NORA: You're like the others. You think I've never had any worries.

MRS. LINDE: Nora dear, you've just told me about all your difficulties—

NORA (*softly*): I haven't told you half of it.

MRS. LINDE: What do you mean?

NORA: I know you look down on me, Christine. But you shouldn't, you know. You're proud that you've worked so hard for your mother.

MRS. LINDE: I'm sure I don't look down on anybody, Nora. But it's true what you say. I am both proud and happy when I think of what I did for my mother. I think I have every right to be.

NORA: Yes, you do. I also have something to be proud and happy about.

MRS. LINDE: What do you mean?

NORA: Speak quietly! Suppose Torvald should hear. Nobody must know about it, Christine.

MRS. LINDE: But what is it?

NORA: I was the one who saved Torvald's life.

MRS. LINDE: Saved his—? How?

NORA: I told you about our trip to Italy. Torvald couldn't have lived if he hadn't gone.

MRS. LINDE: Yes, well, your father gave you the money.

NORA (*smiling*): That's what Torvald and everyone else thinks. But Daddy didn't give us a penny. It was I who found the money.

MRS. LINDE: You? All of it?

NORA: Twelve hundred dollars.

MRS. LINDE: Where did you get it from? You couldn't have borrowed it.

NORA: Why not?

MRS. LINDE: Well, a wife can't borrow money without her husband's consent.

NORA: Ah, but when a wife has a little business sense . . . when she knows how to be clever . . .

MRS. LINDE: I simply don't understand—

NORA: You don't have to. No one has said I borrowed the money. I might have gotten it some other way, perhaps from an admirer.

MRS. LINDE: Don't be so silly! You haven't done anything foolish, have you?

NORA: Is it foolish to save your husband's life?

MRS. LINDE: I think it's foolish if, without his knowledge, you—

NORA: But the whole point was that he mustn't know anything. He wasn't even to know how seriously ill he was. I was the one they told that his life was in danger. The only way to save him was to go to a warmer climate for a while. Don't you think I tried to talk him into it at first? I told him how wonderful it would be for me to go abroad like other young wives. I even suggested that he take out a loan. Then he got angry with me. He said I was being frivolous. All right, I thought; somehow you've got to be saved. Then I thought of a way—

MRS. LINDE: But didn't he find out that the money hadn't come from your father?

NORA: No. Daddy died just about at that time.

MRS. LINDE: And you've never told your husband about this?

NORA: For heaven's sake, no! Torvald is so strict about such matters. Besides, he's so proud of being a *man*. It would be painful and humiliating for him to learn he owed me anything. It would spoil everything between us.

MRS. LINDE: Will you ever tell him?

NORA (*half-smiling*): Yes—sometime, perhaps. Years from now, when I'm no longer pretty, it might be a good thing to have something up my sleeve. Well, what do you think, Christine? I'm not completely useless, am I? Mind you, all this has caused me a lot of worry. It hasn't always been easy for me to meet my obligations. I've had to save a little here and there, wherever I could.

MRS. LINDE: Poor Nora! So it had to come out of your own allowance?

NORA: Whenever Torvald gives me money to buy myself new clothes, I use only half of it. And I always buy the plainest things.

MRS. LINDE: How much have you been able to pay off?

NORA: Well, I can't say exactly. It's hard to keep track of where you are in dealings like this. All I know is that I've paid off as much as I could scrape together. Sometimes, I really didn't know where to turn. (*Smiles*) Then I'd sit here and imagine some rich old gentleman had fallen in love with me—

MRS. LINDE: What! What gentleman?

NORA: —and when he died, they would open his will, and it would say in big letters: "Everything I own is to be paid to the charming Mrs. Nora Helmer."

MRS. LINDE: But my dear Nora—who *is* this man?

NORA: Great heavens, don't you understand? There is no old gentleman. He was something I used to dream up when I didn't know where to turn next for money.

(*The doorbell is heard in the hall.*)

MRS. LINDE (*getting up*): There's the bell. Perhaps I'd better go.

NORA: No, stay. It won't be for me.

Scene 3

The same room. The MAID *enters, followed shortly by* NILS KROGSTAD.

MAID (*in the doorway*): Excuse me, madam. A gentleman is here to see Mr. Helmer. I didn't quite know what to do—the doctor is in there.

NORA: Who is this gentleman?

KROGSTAD (*in the doorway*): It's me, Mrs. Helmer.

(MRS. LINDE *faces him and then turns away toward the window.*)

NORA (*taking a step toward him and speaking in a whisper*): You? What is it? What do you want to talk to my husband about?

KROGSTAD: Business—you might call it. I hold a minor job at the bank. I hear your husband is to become the new manager.

NORA: Oh—then it isn't—?

KROGSTAD: Pure business, Mrs. Helmer. Nothing more.

NORA: Well, you'll find him in his study.

(*She nods and shuts the hall door behind him. Then she walks across the room to the stove.*)

MRS. LINDE: Nora, who was that man?

NORA: His name is Krogstad.

MRS. LINDE: It *was* him, then.

NORA: Do you know him?

MRS. LINDE: I used to know him some years ago. He was a clerk in our district for a while. How he's changed!

NORA: His marriage wasn't a very happy one.

MRS. LINDE: He's a widower now, isn't he?

NORA: Yes, with many children. Ah, now it will burn better.

(*She closes the stove door and moves the rocking chair to one side.*)

MRS. LINDE: He does various things now, I hear?

NORA: Does he? It's quite possible. But let's not talk about business. It's so boring.

(Dr. Rank *enters from* Helmer's *study.*)

Dr. Rank: No, no, I won't intrude, Torvald. I'll go and have a word with your wife. (*Closes the door and notices* Mrs. Linde) Oh, I beg your pardon. I'm afraid I'm intruding here as well.

Nora: No, not at all. Dr. Rank, meet Mrs. Linde.

Rank: Ah! A name I've often heard mentioned in this house. I believe I passed you on the stairs.

Mrs. Linde: Yes. I have to take them slowly.

Rank: Oh, have you hurt yourself?

Mrs. Linde: No, I'm just a little run-down.

Rank: Is that all? Then I suppose you've come to town to cure yourself with a round of parties?

Mrs. Linde: I have come here to find work.

Rank: Is that supposed to be cure for being run-down?

Mrs. Linde: One must live, Doctor.

Rank: Yes, it's generally thought to be necessary.

Nora: Oh, really, Dr. Rank. I think *you* want to stay alive.

Rank: You bet I do. However miserable I sometimes feel, I still want to go on for as long as possible. It's the same with all my patients, too, and with those who are morally sick. There's a bad case of that kind talking with Helmer this minute.

Mrs. Linde (*softly*): Oh!

Nora: Whom do you mean?

RANK: That man, Krogstad. You wouldn't know him. He's rotten to the core. But even he began to talk about having to *live*—as though it were something very important.

NORA: Oh? What did he want to talk to Torvald about?

RANK: Something about the bank.

NORA: I didn't know that Krog—that this Mr. Krogstad had anything to do with the bank.

RANK: Yes, he's got some kind of job down there.

(NORA *laughs to herself and claps her hands.*)

RANK: Why are you laughing?

NORA: Tell me, Dr. Rank, will everyone who works at the bank come under Torvald now?

RANK: Is *that* what you find so very funny?

NORA (*smiling and humming*): Never you mind! Yes, I find it very amusing to think that we— I mean Torvald—now has power over so many people. (*She takes a bag out of her pocket.*) Dr. Rank, would you like a small cookie?

RANK: Cookies! I thought they were forbidden here.

NORA: Yes, but these are some Christine gave me.

MRS. LINDE: What? I—?

NORA: Now, now, don't worry. You weren't to know that Torvald has forbidden them. He's afraid they'll ruin my teeth. Still . . . what does it matter once in a while! Don't you think so, Dr. Rank? Here! (*She pops a cookie into his mouth.*) You too, Christine. I shall have one as well. Just a little one. Two at the most. (*Begins to walk around again*) Yes, now I feel really happy. There's one thing in the world I'd love to do . . .

RANK: Here he comes!

NORA (*hiding the bag of cookies*): Sh! Sh!

(HELMER *comes out of his study, carrying his coat and hat.*)

NORA: Well, Torvald dear, did you get rid of him?

HELMER: Yes, he's gone.

NORA: May I introduce you? This is Christine. She's just arrived in town . . .

HELMER: Christine? Forgive me, but I don't think—

NORA: Mrs. Linde, Torvald dear. Christine Linde.

HELMER: Ah, indeed? A school friend of my wife, I presume?

MRS. LINDE: Yes, we knew each other in earlier days.

NORA: Imagine, now; she's come all this way just to have a word with you.

HELMER: Oh?

MRS. LINDE: Well, I didn't really—

NORA: You see, Christine is very good at office work. She's very keen to come under some really clever man so that she can learn even more.

HELMER: Very sensible, madam.

NORA: She heard you'd become head of the bank. It was in her local paper. So she came here as quickly as she could. Torvald, you will try to do something for her, for my sake?

HELMER: Well, that shouldn't be impossible. You are a widow, I presume?

MRS. LINDE: Yes.

HELMER: You have experience in office work?

MRS. LINDE: Yes, quite a bit.

HELMER: Well, then, it's quite likely I may be able to find a job for you—

NORA (*clapping her hands*): You see, you see!

HELMER: You have come at a fortunate moment.

MRS. LINDE: Oh, how can I ever thank you—?

HELMER: Not at all. (*He puts on his overcoat.*) But for now, I'm afraid I must ask you to excuse me.

RANK: Wait. I'll come with you.

NORA: Don't be long, Torvald dear.

HELMER: I'll only be an hour.

NORA: Are you going too, Christine?

MRS. LINDE (*putting on her coat*): Yes, I must start to look around for a room.

HELMER: Perhaps we can all walk down the road together.

NORA: It's such a nuisance that we're so crowded here. I'm afraid we can't offer to—

MRS. LINDE: Oh, I wouldn't dream of it. Good-bye, Nora dear, and thanks for everything.

NORA: Good-bye for now. But you'll be coming back this evening, of course—and you, too, Dr. Rank. What? If you're well enough? Of course you'll be well enough. Wrap yourself warmly.

(*They go out, talking, into the hall. Children's voices are heard from the stairs.*)

NORA: Here they are! Here they are!

(*She runs out and opens the front door. Anne Marie, the* NURSEMAID, *enters with the children.*)

NORA: Come in, come in! (*Stoops down and kisses them*) Oh, my sweet darlings! Look at them, Christine! Aren't they lovely?

RANK: Don't stand here chattering in this draft!

HELMER: Come along, Mrs. Linde. This place is now unbearable for anybody but mothers.

(Dr. RANK, HELMER, *and* MRS. LINDE *go down the stairs. The* NURSEMAID *brings the children into the room.* NORA *closes the door to the hall.*)

Scene 4

The same room. NORA, *and the children enter.*

NORA: How well you look! What red cheeks you have! Like apples and roses! (*The children chatter away as she talks to them.*) Have you had fun? That's splendid. You gave Emmy and Bob a ride on the sled? Both together? That's a clever boy, Ivar. Oh, let me hold her for a moment, Anne Marie! My sweet little baby doll! (*Takes Emmy from the* NURSEMAID *and dances with her*) All right, Mommy will dance with Bobby, too. No, don't bother, Anne Marie. I'll help them off with their things. Go inside and warm yourself. You look frozen. (*The* NURSEMAID *goes into the room on the left.*) You mustn't touch the packages, Ivar! Shall we play something? Hide and seek? Yes. Me first? All right, I'll hide first.

(*She and the children play, laughing and shouting. Meanwhile, there has been a knock on the front door, which nobody has heard. The door opens, and* KROGSTAD *enters.*)

KROGSTAD: Excuse me, Mrs. Helmer—

NORA (*surprised*): Oh! What do *you* want?

KROGSTAD: I beg your pardon. The front door was unlocked.

NORA (*standing up*): My husband isn't at home.

KROGSTAD: I know.

NORA: Well, what do you want here, then?

KROGSTAD: A word with you.

NORA: With . . . ? (*To the children, quietly*) Go to Anne Marie. When the man is gone, we'll have another game. (*She takes the children into the other room and shuts the door behind them.*) You want to speak to me?

KROGSTAD: Yes.

NORA: Today? But it isn't the first of the month.

KROGSTAD: No, it's Christmas Eve. Whether or not you have a merry Christmas depends on you.

NORA: But I can't give you anything today—

KROGSTAD: Let's not talk about that for the moment. It's something else. I was sitting in the café down the street when I saw your husband go by with a lady.

NORA: So?

KROGSTAD: Might I be so bold as to ask whether that lady was a Mrs. Linde?

NORA: Yes.

KROGSTAD: Just arrived in town?

NORA: Yes, today.

KROGSTAD: She's a good friend of yours?

NORA: Yes, she is. But I don't see—

KROGSTAD: I used to know her once, too.

NORA: I know.

KROGSTAD: Oh? You've discovered that. Yes, I thought you would have. Well then, may I ask you a straight question? Is Mrs. Linde getting a job at the bank?

NORA: How dare you question me like this, Mr. Krogstad? You, one of my husband's employees? But since you ask, yes, Mrs. Linde *is* to be employed at the bank, and I arranged it.

KROGSTAD: So I guessed right then.

NORA (*pacing around the room*): Oh, one has a little influence, you know. Just because one happens to be a woman, that doesn't mean . . . When one is in a humble position, Mr. Krogstad, one should think twice before offending someone who—

KROGSTAD: —who has influence?

NORA: Exactly.

KROGSTAD (*changing his tone*): Mrs. Helmer, will you have the kindness to use your influence on my behalf?

NORA: What? What do you mean?

KROGSTAD: Will you be so good as to see that I keep my humble position at the bank?

NORA: What do you mean? Who is thinking of removing you from your position?

KROGSTAD: You need not pretend you don't know. I realize whom I have to thank for being pushed out like this.

NORA: But I assure you . . .

KROGSTAD: There's still time. I advise you to use your influence to stop it.

NORA: But, Mr. Krogstad, I have no influence!

KROGSTAD: Oh? I thought you just said—

NORA: I didn't mean it that way. How on earth could you imagine that I would have any influence over my husband?

KROGSTAD: Oh, I've known your husband since we were students together. I imagine he has his weaknesses like other married men.

NORA: If you insult my husband like that, I shall show you the door.

KROGSTAD: You're a bold woman, Mrs. Helmer.

NORA: I'm not frightened of you any more. Once the New Year is here, I'll soon be rid of you.

KROGSTAD (*more controlled*): Listen to me, Mrs. Helmer. If forced to, I shall fight for my little job at the bank as if I were fighting for my life.

NORA: So it seems.

KROGSTAD: It isn't just the money. There's something else. You know, of course, as everyone else does, that some years ago I got mixed up in a bit of trouble.

NORA: I think I did hear something—

KROGSTAD: It never went to court. But right away, it was as if all job openings were barred to me. So I turned to the kind of business you know about. But now I have to get out of it. My sons are growing up. For their sake, I have to get back what respectability I can. The job in the bank was the first step on the ladder for me. Now your husband wants to kick me off the ladder and back into the dirt.

NORA: But my dear Mr. Krogstad, it simply isn't in my power to help you.

KROGSTAD: You say that because you don't want to help me. But I have ways of making you.

NORA: You don't mean you'd tell my husband that I owe you money?

KROGSTAD: And if I did?

NORA: That would be a rotten shame! (*Almost in tears*) You would make things very unpleasant for me.

KROGSTAD: Just unpleasant?

NORA (*angrily*): All right, do it! You will be the one to suffer. It will show my husband the kind of man you are. Then you'll never keep your job. He will pay you whatever is owed right away, and we shall have nothing more to do with you.

KROGSTAD (*taking a step closer to her*): Listen, Mrs. Helmer. Either you have a bad memory, or else you don't understand much about business.

NORA: What do you mean?

KROGSTAD: When your husband was ill, you came to me for a loan. Twelve hundred dollars.

NORA: I didn't know anyone else.

KROGSTAD: I promised to find that sum for you on certain conditions. I promised to get you the money in exchange for an IOU which I drew up.

NORA: Yes, and which I signed.

KROGSTAD: Exactly. But then I added a few lines naming your father as security for the debt. This paragraph was to be signed by your father.

NORA: Was to? He did sign it.

KROGSTAD: I had left the date blank. Your father was to add the date himself when he signed it. Remember?

NORA: Yes, I think so.

KROGSTAD: Your father was very ill at the time, I believe.

NORA: He was dying.

KROGSTAD: He died a short time later?

NORA: Yes.

KROGSTAD: Tell me, Mrs. Helmer. Do you remember the exact date your father died?

NORA: September 29.

KROGSTAD: Quite correct. I took the trouble to look into it. Now that leaves me with a curious little problem—which I simply cannot solve. (*Takes out a paper*) The curious thing is that your father signed the document three days after his death.

NORA: What? I don't understand—?

KROGSTAD: Look here. Your father has dated his signature October 2. Isn't that rather strange, Mrs. Helmer? (NORA *remains silent.*) It's also strange that the date is not in your father's handwriting. It's in a handwriting that is familiar to me. Well, your father could have forgotten to date his signature. Someone might have made a guess at the date later on. What really matters is the signature. It is genuine, isn't it, Mrs. Helmer? It was your father who wrote his name here?

NORA (*throwing her head back defiantly*): No, it was not. It was I who wrote Father's name.

KROGSTAD: Do you realize that this is a dangerous admission?

NORA: Why? You'll soon get your money.

KROGSTAD: May I ask you a question? Why didn't you send the document to your father?

NORA: I couldn't. Daddy was ill. And I would have had to explain what the money was for. But I couldn't have told him in his condition that my husband's life was in danger. I couldn't have done that.

KROGSTAD: But didn't it occur to you that you were being dishonest toward me?

NORA: I couldn't bother about that.

KROGSTAD: Mrs. Helmer, it's quite clear that you still don't understand what you've done. I can assure you that it's no worse a crime than the one I once committed, and that crime ruined my whole reputation.

NORA: You? Do you expect me to believe that you would have taken a risk like that to save your wife's life?

KROGSTAD: The law does not care about motives.

NORA: Then the law must be very stupid.

KROGSTAD: Stupid or not, if I show this paper to the police, you will be judged according to it.

NORA: I don't believe it. Isn't a daughter allowed to save her father from worry on his deathbed? Isn't a wife allowed to try to save her husband's life? It must say somewhere that things like this are allowed. You should know that—you're a lawyer. You can't be a very good lawyer, Mr. Krogstad.

KROGSTAD: I do know something about the kind of business we've done together. So do as you please, Mrs. Helmer. But I tell you this: If I am thrown into the gutter a second time, I shall take you down with me.

(*He bows and goes out through the hall.*)

Scene 5

The same room. NORA *stands alone.*

NORA (*tossing her head*): Rubbish! He's just trying to scare me. I'm not that stupid. (*Gathers up the children's clothes; then stops*) Yet . . . no, it's impossible! I did it for love, didn't I? (*She sits down on the sofa and takes up her embroidery. Then she flings her work down, goes to the door, and calls out.*) Helene! Bring in the Christmas tree!

MAID (*enters with the tree*): Where shall I put it, madam?

NORA: There, in the middle of the room.

MAID: Will you be wanting anything else?

NORA: No, thank you. I have everything I need.

(*The* MAID *puts down the tree and leaves.*)

NORA: Candles here—flowers here. Revolting man! There's nothing to worry about. The Christmas tree must be beautiful.

(HELMER *enters, carrying a bundle of papers.*)

NORA: Oh, are you back already?

HELMER: Yes. Has anybody been here?

NORA: Here? No.

HELMER: That's strange. I just saw Krogstad leave the house.

NORA: Did you? Oh, yes. Krogstad was here for a few minutes.

HELMER: Nora, I can tell from your face that something is wrong. He's been here and asked you to put in a good word for him, hasn't he?

NORA: Yes.

HELMER: And you were to pretend that it was your own idea, correct?

NORA: Yes, Torvald. But . . .

HELMER: Nora, Nora. What made you ever think of doing a thing like that? And then on top of everything, telling me a lie!

NORA: A lie?

HELMER: Didn't you say that nobody had been here? (*Wags his finger*) My little songbird must never do that again. Let's say no more about it. (*Sits down by the stove*) Ah, nice and cozy! (*He glances through his papers.*)

NORA (*busy with the Christmas tree*): Are you very busy, Torvald? What are those papers?

HELMER: Just something to do with the bank.

NORA: Already?

HELMER: I persuaded the retiring manager to let me make some changes right away in the bank's staff and organization. I want to have everything straight by the New Year.

NORA: Then that's why this poor man Krogstad—

HELMER: Hmm.

NORA (*leaning on his chair, running her fingers through his hair*): If you hadn't been so busy, I was going to ask you a big favor.

HELMER: Well, tell me.

NORA: I'm so looking forward to the fancy dress ball at the Stenborgs the night after Christmas. I want to look my best. You know I trust your taste more than anyone's. Couldn't you give me some advice on what kind of costume I should wear?

HELMER: Very well, I'll think about it. We'll find something.

NORA: That's kind of you. (*Goes back to the tree; pause*) How pretty these red flowers look. Tell me. Was it really something very bad that Krogstad did?

HELMER: He forged someone's name. Have you any idea what that means?

NORA: Might he have been forced to do it because of some emergency?

HELMER: Maybe. I'm not so heartless to condemn a man for a single mistake.

NORA: Oh no, Torvald. Of course not!

HELMER: Men often succeed in getting back their reputations if they admit their crime and take their punishment.

NORA: Punishment?

HELMER: But Krogstad didn't do that. He tried to trick his way out of it. That's what morally destroyed him. Just think how a man with that on his conscience will have to behave. He will always have to lie and cheat. He can never drop the mask, not even with his wife and children. Yes, the children—*that's* the worst part of it, Nora.

NORA: Why?

HELMER: Lies spread disease and infection to every part of a household. Every breath the children draw in such a house contains the germs of evil.

NORA: Do you really believe that?

HELMER: Oh, my dear. I've come across it often in my line of work. Nearly all young criminals are the children of mothers who are dishonest.

NORA: Why do you say mothers?

HELMER: It's usually the mother, though the father can have the same influence. Every lawyer knows that only too well. Yet, this fellow Krogstad has been sitting at home all these years poisoning his children with his lies and deceit. That's why I say that, morally speaking, he is dead. (*Stretches out his hands to her*) So my pretty little Nora must promise not to try to put in a good word for him. Give me your hand on it. There now! That's settled.

NORA (*drawing her hand away and walking over to the other side of the Christmas tree*): How hot it is in here! And I've so much to do.

HELMER (*standing up and collecting his papers*): Yes, and I must try to get some of this read before dinner. I must also think about your costume, my precious little songbird!

(*He goes into his study and closes the door.*)

NORA (*softly, after a pause*): It's nonsense! It can't be. It's impossible! It *must* be impossible.

NURSEMAID (*in the doorway*): The children are asking if they can come in to Mummy.

NORA: No, no, no. Don't let them in! You stay with them, Anne Marie.

NURSEMAID: Very good, madam. (*Closes the door*)

NORA (*pale with fear*): Corrupt my children . . . poison my home! (*Short pause; throws back her head*) It isn't true! It *couldn't* be true.

(*Curtain*)

ACT 2

This act takes place on Christmas day. Nora asks for Mrs. Linde's help in repairing the costume she must wear to a fancy party the following night. Nora tells Mrs. Linde that Dr. Rank is seriously ill. Mrs. Linde mistakenly believes that Dr. Rank is the person who loaned Nora the $1,200 years before.

Nora once again asks Torvald not to fire Krogstad from his job at the bank. Torvald becomes annoyed. He immediately sends a letter to Krogstad telling him of his dismissal.

Krogstad tells Nora that he will keep her IOU as blackmail. As he goes out, he leaves Torvald a letter explaining Nora's forgery. Nora decides that she has until the end of the party—31 more hours—left to live.

Scene 1

The same room. In the corner beside the piano stands the Christmas tree. It is stripped, ragged, and has its candles burned out. NORA'S *outdoor clothes lie on the sofa. She is alone in the room, walking restlessly back and forth.*

NORA: There's someone coming! (*Goes to the door and listens*) No, it's no one. Of course, no one will come today. It's Christmas Day. Nor tomorrow either. But perhaps . . . (*Opens the door and looks out*) No, nothing in the letter box. (*Walks across the room*) Silly, silly. Of course he won't do anything. It couldn't happen. It's impossible. Why, I have three small children.

(*The* NURSEMAID *enters carrying a big cardboard box.*)

NURSEMAID: I found those fancy dress clothes at last, madam.

NORA: Thank you. Put them on the table.

NURSEMAID: I'm afraid they're in an awful mess.

NORA: Oh, I wish I could tear them into a million pieces!

NURSEMAID: Why, madam! They'll be all right. They just need a little mending.

NORA: Yes, I'll get Mrs. Linde to help me. How are the children?

NURSEMAID: Playing with their Christmas presents, poor little dears. But they're so used to being with their Mummy.

NORA: Yes. But Anne Marie, from now on I can't be with them as often as I was before.

NURSEMAID: Well, children get used to anything in time.

NORA: Do you think so? Do you think they'd forget their mother if she went away forever?

NURSEMAID: Good heavens—forever!

NORA: Tell me, Anne Marie. I've often wondered how you could bear to give your child away—to strangers?

NURSEMAID: Well, I had to when I came to nurse my little Nora.

NORA: Do you mean you wanted to?

NURSEMAID: I had the chance at such a good job. A poor girl who has troubles can't afford to pick and choose. *He* certainly didn't help at all.

NORA: But your daughter must have completely forgotten you.

NURSEMAID: Oh, no she hasn't. She's written to me twice.

NORA (*hugging her*): Dear old Anne Marie. You were such a good mother to me when I was little.

NURSEMAID: My poor little Nora never had any mother but me.

NORA: And if my little ones only had you, I know you would . . . Oh, what am I talking about! (*She opens the box.*) Go into them. Tomorrow, you'll see how pretty I am going to look.

NURSEMAID: Why, they'll be nobody at the ball as beautiful as my Miss Nora. (*She exits.*)

NORA (*begins to unpack the clothes from the box, but soon throws them down again*): Oh, if only I dared go out! If I could be sure no one would come. (*Cries out*) Ah—they're coming! (MRS. LINDE *enters from the hall.*) Oh, it's you, Christine. I'm so glad you're here. There's something you must help me with. You see, there's going to be a fancy dress ball tomorrow night upstairs at the Stenborgs. Torvald wants me to go as an

Italian fisher-girl and dance the tarantella. I learned it in Capri, you know. Look, here's the costume. Torvald had it made for me down there. But it's all torn—

MRS. LINDE: Oh, I can fix that. The stitching has just come away.

NORA: It's awfully kind of you.

MRS. LINDE (*sewing*): So you are going to be all dressed up tomorrow, Nora? I must pop over for a minute to see how you look. And I've forgotten to thank you for the pleasant time we had last night. But tell me, is Dr. Rank always as depressed as he was last night?

NORA: Not really. He's very ill, you know. He has tuberculosis of the spine, poor man.

MRS. LINDE: Does Dr. Rank visit you every day?

NORA: Every day. He's Torvald's oldest friend and a good friend to me, too. Dr. Rank is almost one of the family.

MRS. LINDE: When you introduced me to him yesterday, he said he'd often heard my name mentioned in this house. But later I noticed your husband had no idea who I was. So how could Dr. Rank—?

NORA: Yes, that's quite right, Christine. You see Torvald is so in love with me that he wants me all to himself. Those are his very words. It used to make him jealous if I even mentioned any of my old friends back home. So, naturally, I stopped talking about them. But I often chat with Dr. Rank about such things. He enjoys it more.

MRS. LINDE: Now listen, Nora. I'm a bit older than you and know more of the world. You ought to give up this business with Dr. Rank.

NORA: What business?

MRS. LINDE: The whole thing. Last night you were speaking about this rich admirer of yours who was going to give you money—

NORA: One who doesn't exist, I regret to say.

MRS. LINDE: Is Dr. Rank rich?

NORA: Yes.

MRS. LINDE: And he has no dependents?

NORA: No, no one. But—I don't understand.

MRS. LINDE: How dare a man of his position be so forward?

NORA: What on earth are you talking about?

MRS. LINDE: Stop pretending, Nora. Do you think I don't know who you borrowed the money from?

NORA: Are you out of your mind? How could you imagine such a thing? A friend, someone who comes here every day! Why, that would be an impossible situation!

MRS. LINDE: It really wasn't him, then?

NORA: No, of course not. It would never have occurred to me to ask Dr. Rank. Though I'm sure that if I ever did ask him—

MRS. LINDE: Behind your husband's back?

NORA: I must get out of this other business, which *has* been going on behind his back.

MRS. LINDE: Yes, that's what I said yesterday.

NORA (*walking up and down*): When you've paid everything you owe, do you get your IOU back?

MRS. LINDE: Yes, of course.

NORA: And you can tear it into a thousand pieces—and burn the nasty, filthy thing?

MRS. LINDE (*putting down her sewing*): Nora, something has happened since yesterday morning. What is it?

NORA: Christine! (*Listens*) Sh! There's Torvald. Would you mind going to sit with the children for a few minutes? Torvald can't bear to see sewing lying around. Get Anne Marie to help you.

MRS. LINDE (*gathering things together*): All right. But I won't leave this house until we've talked this matter out. (*She exits as* HELMER *enters from the hall.*)

NORA: Oh, Torvald dear. I've been longing for you to return.

HELMER: Was that the dressmaker?

NORA: No, it was Christine. She's helping me with my costume. I think it's going to look very nice. Have you got work to do?

HELMER: Yes. (*Shows her a bundle of papers*) Look at these. (*Turns to go to his study*)

NORA: Torvald.

HELMER (*stopping*): Yes.

NORA: If a little squirrel asked you really nicely to grant her a wish—would you?

HELMER: First I would have to know what it was. I hope it isn't that business you were talking about this morning?

NORA (*approaching* HELMER): Yes, it is, Torvald. I beg of you!

HELMER: You have the nerve to bring that up again?

NORA: Yes, yes, you must listen to me. You must let Krogstad keep his job at the bank.

HELMER: But I'm giving his job to Mrs. Linde.

NORA: Yes, that's awfully sweet of you. But couldn't you get rid of one of the other clerks instead of Krogstad?

HELMER: You're being incredibly stubborn. Just because you made a thoughtless promise to him, you expect me to . . .

NORA: No, it isn't that, Torvald. It's for your own sake. That man writes in the most awful newspapers. You said so yourself. He can do you great harm. I'm frightened of him.

HELMER: Oh, I understand. Memories of the past. That's what's frightening you.

NORA: What do you mean?

HELMER: You're thinking of your father.

NORA: Yes, yes, that's right. Remember all those horrible things men wrote in the papers about Father? I honestly think they would have fired him if you hadn't been sent to investigate. You were so kind and helpful to him.

HELMER: My dear little Nora. There is a great deal of difference between your father and me. Your father's behavior at work was not completely above suspicion. Mine is. And I hope it remains that way for as long as I hold this position.

NORA: But no one knows what spiteful people may think up. That's why I beg of you—

HELMER: Everyone down at the bank already knows that I intend to dismiss Krogstad. If it ever got around that the new manager had been persuaded by his wife to change his mind—

NORA: What of it?

HELMER: I refuse to make a laughingstock of myself in front of the entire staff. Anyway, there's another reason why it is impossible for Krogstad to stay on while I am manager.

NORA: What is that?

HELMER: We knew each other rather well when we were younger. Now he makes no attempt to hide that fact, especially when others are present. He thinks he has every right to treat me as an equal. It's 'Torvald this' or

'Torvald that' every time he opens his mouth. I find it very annoying. He would make my position at the bank very difficult.

NORA: Torvald, that's so petty.

HELMER: Petty? You think I'm petty? Well, we'll put a stop to that once and for all. (*He opens the door and calls out.*) Helene!

NORA: What are you going to do?

HELMER (*searching among his papers*): Settle things. (*The* MAID *comes in.*) Take this letter downstairs at once. Find a messenger, and see that he delivers it immediately!

MAID: Very good, sir. (*She exits, with the letter.*)

HELMER (*putting his papers together*): Now, my stubborn little miss.

NORA (*breathlessly*): What was in that letter?

HELMER: Krogstad's dismissal.

NORA: Call her back, Torvald! There's still time! Please, for my sake, for your sake, for the sake of the children. You don't realize what you've done!

HELMER: It's too late.

NORA: Yes, it is too late.

HELMER: To think that I should be frightened by anything that miserable penpusher could write. But I forgive you for this craziness. It's a rather sweet way of showing me how much you love me. (*He takes her in his arms.*) When a real crisis comes, you will

45

find I've enough strength and courage for whatever happens. You'll find I'm man enough to take everything on myself.

NORA (*in control of herself*): I shall never let you do that.

HELMER: Very well. We shall share it, Nora—as man and wife. That is as it should be. Now, you go ahead and do your tarantella. Practice with your tambourine. I'll sit in my study and close the door. Then you can make all the noise you want. (*Turns in the doorway*) When Dr. Rank comes, tell him where to find me.

(*He goes into his study and closes the door.*)

Scene 2

The same room. Early evening. Darkness begins to spread over the room.

NORA (*whispering in terror*): He said he'd do it. He will do it, and nothing will stop him. No, never that. I'd rather anything. There must be some way out! (*The doorbell rings in the hall.*) Dr. Rank! (*She pulls herself together and opens the door to the hall.* DR. RANK *is standing there, hanging up his coat.*) Hello, Dr. Rank. Do you mind not going into Torvald just yet. I think he's busy.

RANK: And you? (*He enters the room, and* NORA *closes the door behind him.*)

NORA: Oh, you know very well I've always got time to talk to you.

RANK: Thank you. That is a privilege I will take advantage of for as long as I can.

NORA: What do you mean? Is something going to happen?

RANK: Something I've been expecting for a long time. But I didn't think it would come this soon.

NORA (*seizing his arm*): Tell me, what is it?

RANK: I'm slowly sinking, and there's nothing to be done about it.

NORA (*sighing with relief*): Oh, it's you—?

RANK: Who else? No, it's no good lying to oneself. Within a month I may be rotting up there in the churchyard.

NORA: What a nasty way to talk!

RANK: The facts aren't exactly nice. And the worst is yet to come. I want to ask you a favor. Helmer is a sensitive soul. He hates anything ugly. I don't want him to visit me when I'm in the hospital—

NORA: But Dr. Rank . . .

RANK: I don't want him there for any reason. As soon as I know the worst, I'll send you my visiting card with a black cross on it. Then you'll know the final filthy process has begun.

NORA: Really, you're being quite impossible this evening. And I was hoping you would be in a very good mood.

RANK: With death staring me in the face?

NORA (*putting both her hands on his shoulders*): Dear, dear Dr. Rank. You mustn't die and leave Torvald and me.

RANK: You wouldn't miss me for long. Once one is gone, one is soon forgotten.

NORA (*anxiously*): Do you think so?

RANK: One finds replacements, and then—

NORA: Who will find a replacement?

RANK: You and Helmer both will. You seem to have made a start already, haven't you? What was that Mrs. Linde doing here last night?

NORA: Surely you aren't jealous of poor Christine?

RANK: Yes, I am. She will be my successor in this house when I'm done for.

NORA: Hush! Don't speak so loud. She's in there!

RANK: You see!

NORA: She has just come to mend my dress. Good heavens, how unreasonable you are! (*Sits on the sofa*) Be nice now, Dr. Rank. Tomorrow, you'll see how lovely I can dance. You can pretend I'm doing it just for you—and for Torvald as well, of course. (*She takes some things out of the box.*) Come here, Dr. Rank. I want to show you something.

RANK (*sitting*): Hmm. Silk stockings.

NORA: Aren't they lovely? Why are you looking so critical? Don't you think they will fit me?

RANK: I couldn't give you an expert opinion on that.

NORA: Shame on you! You are too naughty. (*She hits him lightly on the ear with the stockings and puts them in the box.*)

RANK (*after a short pause*): Sitting here like this with you, I can't imagine what would have become of me if I had never come to this house.

NORA (*smiling*): You *do* enjoy coming here.

RANK (*in a low voice, looking straight ahead*): And now to have to say good-bye to it all, and not to be able to leave behind even the slightest token of gratitude. Hardly even a passing sense of loss. Only an empty place, to be filled by the first person that comes along.

NORA: Suppose I were to ask you to—? No—

RANK: What?

NORA: To give me proof of your friendship.

RANK: Yes, yes?

NORA: I mean . . . to do me a very great favor.

RANK: Would you for once grant me that happiness?

NORA: But you have no idea what it is.

RANK: Very well then; tell me.

NORA: It's too much to ask really. I need your advice. And I need you to do something for me.

RANK: The more the better. I've no idea what it can be. But tell me. You do trust me, don't you?

NORA: Yes, more than anyone. You're my best and most faithful friend. Otherwise, I couldn't tell you. There's something I want you to help me prevent. You know how much Torvald loves me. He wouldn't hesitate for a moment to lay down his life for me.

RANK (*leaning towards her*): Nora—do you think he is the only one who would gladly lay down his life for you?

NORA (*sadly*): Oh, Dr. Rank, please don't . . .

RANK: I promised myself I would tell you that before I went. I'll never have a better opportunity. Well, now you know. And now you also know that you can trust me as you can trust nobody else.

NORA (*rising and speaking calmly*): Let me pass, please.

RANK: Nora . . .

NORA (*in the doorway to the hall*): Helene, bring the lamp. (*Goes over to the stove*) Oh, dear Dr. Rank, that was rather horrible of you.

RANK (*getting up*): That I have loved you as deeply as anyone else has? Was that horrible of me?

NORA: No—but that you should go and tell me. That was so unnecessary—

RANK: What do you mean? Did you know, then?

(*The* MAID *enters with the lamp. She puts it on the table and leaves.*)

RANK: Nora—Mrs. Helmer—I am asking, did you know?

NORA: Oh, what did I know? What didn't I know? I really can't say. Oh, how could you be so clumsy, Dr. Rank? Everything was so nice.

RANK: But you know that I'm at your service, body and soul. So you can speak out.

NORA: After this? I can't tell you anything now.

RANK: Yes, yes. You can't punish me like this. Let me do what I can for you.

NORA: You can't do anything for me now. Anyway, I don't need any help. It's all just my imagination, really it is. Of course! (*She sits down in the rocking chair and smiles.*) Well, I must say, Dr. Rank, you are a fine gentleman. Aren't you ashamed of yourself, now that the lamp has been brought in?

RANK: No, not exactly. But perhaps I should go—for good?

NORA: No, you must not do that. You must keep coming just as you've always done. You know quite well how Torvald depends on your company.

RANK: And you?

NORA: I always think it's great fun having you here.

RANK: That's exactly what gave me wrong ideas. You're a riddle to me. I've often thought you'd just as soon be with me as with Helmer.

NORA: Well, there are those people you love and those people you'd almost rather *be* with.

RANK: Oh yes, there is some truth in that.

NORA: When I was a girl at home, I loved Daddy best, of course. But I always enjoyed talking to the servants. They never told me what I had to do, and they were such fun to listen to.

RANK: Ah, I see. I've taken their place.

NORA: Oh, dear, sweet Dr. Rank. I didn't mean that at all. But I'm sure you understand. I feel the same about Torvald as I did about Daddy.

MAID (*enters from the hall*): Excuse me, madam.

(*The* MAID *whispers to* NORA *and hands her a visiting card.* NORA *glances at it and puts it in her pocket.*)

NORA: Oh, my!

RANK: Anything wrong?

NORA: No, not at all. It's just that my new costume has arrived.

RANK: I thought your costume was in *that* box.

NORA: That one, yes. But this is another one. I've ordered it special. Torvald must not know.

RANK: Ah, so that's your big secret?

NORA: Yes, yes. Go in and talk to him, will you? He's in the study. Keep him busy for a bit—

RANK: Don't worry. He won't get away from me.
  (*Goes into Helmer's study*)

NORA (*to the* MAID): Is he waiting in the kitchen?

MAID: Yes, madam. He came up the back stairs.

NORA: Didn't you tell him I had a visitor?

MAID: Yes, but he won't go until he's spoken
  with you.

NORA: Show him in, then. But quietly, Helene.
  You must not tell anyone about this. It's a
  surprise for my husband.

Scene 3

The same room. NORA *walks across the room
and bolts the door to* HELMER's *study.*

NORA: It's happening. It's happening after all.
  No, no, it can't happen. It mustn't happen.

(*The* MAID *opens the door from the hall to let in*
KROGSTAD.)

NORA (*approaching him*): Speak quietly. My
  husband is at home.

KROGSTAD: What if he is?

NORA: What do you want from me?

KROGSTAD: I suppose you know I've been fired.

NORA: I couldn't stop it, Mr. Krogstad. I did my
  best for you, but it didn't help.

KROGSTAD: Does your husband love you so
  little? He knows what I can do to you, and
  yet he dares to—

NORA: Surely you don't think I told him?

KROGSTAD: No, I didn't really think so. It wouldn't have been like my old friend Torvald Helmer to show that much courage—

NORA: Mr. Krogstad. I must ask you to show some respect for my husband.

KROGSTAD: Oh sure, all the respect he deserves. But I know you are very anxious to keep this business quiet, Mrs. Helmer. I take it you now have a clearer idea of just what it is you've done.

NORA: A clearer idea than *you* could have given me. What do you want with me anyway?

KROGSTAD: I just wanted to see how you were. Even somebody like me has feelings, you know.

NORA: Show some then. Think of my children.

KROGSTAD: Have you or your husband thought of mine? Well, let's forget that. There was just one thing I wanted to say. I'm not going to take any action for the present.

NORA: Ah, I knew you wouldn't.

KROGSTAD: Everything can be settled in a friendly way. Nobody has to know. We'll keep it among the three of us.

NORA: My husband must never know about this.

KROGSTAD: How can you prevent it? Can you pay off the balance?

NORA: No, not right away.

KROGSTAD: Have you any way of getting hold of the money in the next few days.

NORA: None that I would care to use.

KROGSTAD: Well, it wouldn't have helped anyway. Even if you had the cash right in your hand, you wouldn't have gotten the IOU back from me now.

NORA: What are you going to do with it?

KROGSTAD: Just keep it. No one else need hear of it. So if you are thinking of trying anything desperate, just give up the idea.

NORA: How did you know I was thinking of *that*?

KROGSTAD: Most of us think of *that* to begin with. I did, too. But I didn't have the courage . . .

NORA: Neither have I.

KROGSTAD: It would be a stupid thing to do anyway. I've got a letter to your husband in my pocket here . . .

NORA (*quickly*): He must never see that letter. Tear it up. I'll find the money somehow.

KROGSTAD: Excuse me, Mrs. Helmer. I've just told you . . .

NORA: I don't mean the money I owe you. Let me know how much you want from my husband. I'll find it for you.

KROGSTAD: I want no money from your husband. I just want to get on my feet again, Mrs. Helmer, and *your* husband is going to help me. For 18 months now my record has been clean. All that time it's been hard going. I had to fight my way back, step by step. Now I've

been thrown out in the mud, and I won't
stand for just getting my job back. I want to
get to the top. I want to go back into that
bank with a better position. Your husband
is going to create a new job just for me—

NORA: He'll never do that.

KROGSTAD: Oh, yes, he will. I know him. He
won't dare risk a scandal. And once I'm in
there, you'll see. Within a year, I'll be his
right-hand man. It will be Nils Krogstad
running that bank, not Torvald Helmer.

NORA: I'll never live to see that day! I will find
the courage . . .

KROGSTAD: People don't do that sort of thing,
Mrs. Helmer. There wouldn't be any point to
it, anyway. I'd still have him right in my
pocket.

NORA: Afterwards? When I'm no longer . . .

KROGSTAD: Have you forgotten that your
reputation would be entirely in my hands?
(NORA *looks at him, speechless.*) Well, I've
warned you. Don't do anything silly. When
Helmer has read my letter, he'll get in touch
with me. Good-bye.

(*He goes out through the hall.* NORA *crosses to
the door, opens it slightly, and listens.*)

NORA: He's leaving. He's not going to give him
the letter. That would be impossible! (*A
letter falls into the letter box. Then* KROGSTAD's
footsteps fade away on the stairs.) In the

letter box! There it is! Torvald, Torvald! It's hopeless now.

MRS. LINDE (*entering the room, carrying the costume*): Well, I've done the best I can. Shall we see how it looks? What's wrong? You look upset.

NORA (*in a low, hoarse whisper*): Come here. Do you see that letter? There, look! Through the glass in the letter box.

MRS. LINDE: Yes, yes, I can see it.

NORA: It's from Krogstad.

MRS. LINDE: Nora! It was Krogstad who lent you the money!

NORA: Yes, and now Torvald's going to discover everything.

MRS. LINDE: Believe me. It's best for you both.

NORA: But there's more to it than that. I forged a signature . . .

MRS. LINDE: For heaven's sake—!

NORA: Listen, I want to tell you something, Christine, so you can be my witness. If anything happened to me . . . so that I wasn't here any longer—

MRS. LINDE: Nora, you don't know what you're saying.

NORA: If anyone should say it was Helmer's fault, then you must testify that it isn't true. I alone was responsible for the whole thing. Remember that!

MRS. LINDE: I will. But I don't understand a word of it.

NORA: Oh, how could you understand? A—miracle is about to happen. But something so terrible as well, Christine. Oh, it must *never* happen, not for anything.

MRS. LINDE: I'll go over and talk to Krogstad.

NORA: Don't go near him. He'll only do you harm.

MRS. LINDE: Many years ago he would have done anything for me.

NORA: Him!

MRS. LINDE: Where does he live?

NORA (*reaching in her pocket*): Here is his card. But the letter, the letter!

HELMER (*from his study, knocking on the door*): Nora!

NORA (*crying out in alarm*): What is it?

HELMER: Don't be frightened. We're not coming in. You've locked the door. Are you trying on your costume?

NORA: Yes, yes, I'm trying on my costume. I'm going to look so pretty for you, Torvald.

MRS. LINDE (*quietly*): He lives just around the corner.

NORA: Yes, but it's no use. The letter is in the box, and Torvald has the key.

MRS. LINDE: Krogstad must ask him to send the letter back, unread. He must find some excuse—

NORA: But this is just the time that Torvald opens the box—

MRS. LINDE: You must stop him. Go in and keep him busy. I'll be back as soon as I can.

Scene 4

The same room. NORA *goes over to* HELMER'*s study, opens the door, and peeps in.*

NORA: Torvald!

HELMER (*from the study*): Well, may a man enter his own drawing room again? Come along, Rank, now we'll see. (*In the doorway*) But what's this? Rank led me to expect some great change.

RANK: That's what I thought, too. But I seem to have been mistaken.

NORA: I'm not showing my costume to anybody before tomorrow night.

HELMER: Nora dear, you look tired. You haven't been practicing your dance too hard?

NORA: No. I haven't practiced at all yet.

HELMER: Well, you must.

NORA: Yes, Torvald, I know. But I can't get anywhere without your help. I've completely forgotten everything.

HELMER: Don't worry. We'll polish it up.

NORA: Yes, help me, Torvald. Promise me you will? You must forget everything else this evening. Promise?

HELMER: I promise. This evening I am entirely yours. Oh, but while I remember . . . (*Goes toward the door*)

NORA: What do you want out there?

HELMER: I just want to see if there are any letters.

NORA: No, don't!

HELMER: Why not?

NORA: Because there's nothing there.

HELMER: Well, I'll just make sure.

(*As he moves towards the door,* NORA *runs to the piano and plays the opening bars of the tarantella.*)

NORA: I can't dance tomorrow if I don't practice with you now. Come and play for me, Torvald dear. Correct me, lead me, the way you always do.

HELMER: Very well, if you wish it.

(*He sits down at the piano.* NORA *grabs the tambourine and a long brightly colored shawl from the cardboard box. She wraps the shawl around her and leaps into the center of the room.*)

NORA: Play for me! I want to dance!

(HELMER *plays and* NORA *dances.* Dr. RANK *stands behind* HELMER *at the piano and watches her.*)

HELMER (*playing*): Slower, slower! Not so wild, Nora. (*Stops playing*) No, no. This won't do at all.

RANK: Let me play for her.

HELMER (*standing up*): Yes, would you? Then it will be easier for me to show her the correct way.

(RANK *sits down at the piano and plays.* NORA *dances more and more wildly.* HELMER *stands by the stove, giving her repeated directions. She does not seem to hear him. Her hair comes undone and falls about her shoulders. She pays no attention and goes on dancing.* MRS. LINDE *enters.*)

NORA (*dancing*): See what fun we are having, Christine.

HELMER: But, Nora darling, you're dancing as if your life depended on it.

NORA: It does.

HELMER: Rank, stop it. This is sheer madness. Stop, I say.

(RANK *stops playing and* NORA *comes to a sudden halt.*)

HELMER (*approaching Nora*): It's beyond belief! You have forgotten everything I taught you. I'll have to show you every step.

NORA: Yes, you must go on coaching me. Right up to the last minute. Promise me, Torvald.

HELMER: You can depend on me.

NORA: You must not think of anything but me until after tomorrow. Don't open any letters—don't even open the letter box—

HELMER: Aha, you're still worried about that fellow—

NORA: Yes, yes, I am.

HELMER: I can see from your face that there is already a letter from him in there.

NORA: But you must not read it now. I don't want anything ugly to come between us until it's all over.

HELMER (*putting his arm around her*): The child must have her way. But tomorrow night, when your dance is over—

NORA: Then you will be free.

MAID (*in the doorway*): Dinner is served.

NORA: Put out some champagne, Helene.

MAID: Very good, madam. (*Goes out*)

HELMER: I say! What's this, a banquet?

NORA: We'll drink champagne until dawn! Go ahead inside. I'll be with you in a minute. Christine, you must help me put my hair up.

(HELMER *and* Dr. RANK *exit.*)

NORA: Well?

MRS. LINDE: He's left town. He'll be back tomorrow evening. I left a note for him.

NORA: You shouldn't have done that. Anyway, it's wonderful really in a way—sitting here and waiting for a miracle to happen.

MRS. LINDE: What miracle are you waiting for?

NORA: Oh, you wouldn't understand. Go and join them. I'll be there in a moment.

(MRS. LINDE *goes into the dining room.* NORA *stands for a moment as if to collect herself. Then she looks at her watch.*)

NORA: Five o'clock. Seven hours till midnight, and another 24 hours till midnight tomorrow. Then the tarantella will be over. Twenty-four and seven? Thirty-one hours to live.

HELMER (*in the doorway*): What's happened to my little songbird?

NORA (*running to him with her arms open*): Your songbird is here!

(*Curtain*)

ACT 3

It is the following night. While Torvald, Nora, and Dr. Rank are upstairs at the party, Christine Linde waits alone in the Helmer apartment for Krogstad. Christine tells Krogstad that she has come to town to renew their lost love. He is deeply moved and offers to ask Helmer to return his letter. Christine, however, wants the lies to end in the Helmer household.

After the party, Torvald goes to the mailbox and finds Krogstad's letter. When Torvald rushes into the hall demanding an explanation, Nora reveals how unhappy she has been in their marriage.

Scene 1

The same room. MRS. LINDE *is seated at the table, glancing through a book. She seems unable to keep her mind on it. She turns several times and listens for the front door.*

MRS. LINDE (*looking at her watch*): Still not here. There isn't much time left. I hope he hasn't . . . (*Listens again*) Ah, here he is. (*Footsteps can be heard on the stairs. She whispers.*) Come in. There's nobody here.

KROGSTAD (*in the doorway*): I found a note from you at my house. What does it mean?

MRS. LINDE: I must speak with you.

KROGSTAD: Did it have to be in this house?

MRS. LINDE: We couldn't meet at my place. It doesn't have a separate entrance. Come in.

The maid is asleep, and the Helmers are upstairs.

KROGSTAD: Have we anything to talk about?

MRS. LINDE: We have a great deal to talk about.

KROGSTAD: I wasn't aware of it.

MRS. LINDE: That's because you never understood me.

KROGSTAD: What was there to understand? It's the old story, isn't it? A woman throws a man over when something better comes along.

MRS. LINDE: Do you really think it was easy for me to give you up?

KROGSTAD: Then why did you write to me the way you did?

MRS. LINDE: Because I thought it was my duty to destroy any love you had for me.

KROGSTAD (*clenching his hands*): So that was it. And you did this for money!

MRS. LINDE: You must not forget that I had a helpless mother and two little brothers to take care of. We couldn't wait for you, Nils. It would have been so long before you had enough to support us.

KROGSTAD: Perhaps. But when I lost you, it was as if the ground had slipped out from under me. Look at me now. I am a broken man clinging to the wreck of his life.

MRS. LINDE: Help may be near.

KROGSTAD: It was near. Then you came along and got in the way.

MRS. LINDE: I didn't know. No one told me until today that the job I was given was yours.

KROGSTAD: If you say so, I believe you. But now that you know, will you give it up?

MRS. LINDE: No—because it wouldn't help you even if I did.

KROGSTAD: Maybe not, but *I* would do it just the same.

MRS. LINDE: I have learned to be more careful. Life and poverty have taught me that.

KROGSTAD: Life has taught me not to believe in pretty speeches.

MRS. LINDE: Then it has taught you a useful lesson. But surely you still believe in actions? Listen, I'm in the same position as you are, no one to care about, no one to care for.

KROGSTAD: You made your own choice.

MRS. LINDE: I had no choice—then. But now . . . suppose we two shipwrecked souls joined hands? Lost souls like us have a better chance of survival together than on our own.

KROGSTAD: Christine, are you being serious?

MRS. LINDE: Why do you think I came to town?

KROGSTAD: You mean you came because of me?

MRS. LINDE: I must work to live. But now I'm alone in the world. I feel so very lost and empty. There is no joy in working just for

oneself. Oh, Nils, give me something—
to work for—to live for.

KROGSTAD: I don't believe all this. You're just
being hysterical and romantic.

MRS. LINDE: Have you ever known me to be
hysterical before?

KROGSTAD: Would you really do this? Tell me—
do you know about my past?

MRS. LINDE: Yes.

KROGSTAD: You know what people think of me
here?

MRS. LINDE: Just now you hinted that you might have been a different person with me.

KROGSTAD: I know I could have.

MRS. LINDE: Well, couldn't it still happen?

Krogstad: Christine—have you the courage?

MRS. LINDE: Your children need a mother, and I need people to take care of. Besides, I believe in you, Nils.

KROGSTAD (*grabbing her hands*): Thank you, Christine. Now I can try to make the world believe in me, too . . .

MRS. LINDE (*listening*): Hush! The tarantella! You must go quickly!

KROGSTAD: Why? What is it?

MRS. LINDE: You hear that dance? As soon as it's finished, they'll be coming down.

KROGSTAD: Okay, I'll go. But, Christine, you don't know what I've just done to the Helmers.

MRS. LINDE: Yes, Nils, I do. I know what despair can do to a man like you.

KROGSTAD: Oh, if only I could undo this!

MRS. LINDE: You can. Your letter is still in the box.

KROGSTAD (*looks at her searchingly*): Is that why you're doing this? You want to save your friend at any price? Tell me the truth. Is that the reason?

MRS. LINDE: When you've sold yourself *once* for other people's sake, you don't do it again.

KROGSTAD: Then I shall demand my letter back.

MRS. LINDE: No, no.

KROGSTAD: Of course I will. I'll stay here until Helmer comes down. I'll say the letter was about my dismissal, and that I don't want him to read it.

MRS. LINDE: No, Nils. Don't ask for it back.

KROGSTAD: But—tell me—wasn't that the real reason you asked me to come?

MRS. LINDE: Yes, at first—when I was frightened. But a day has passed since then. In that time, I've seen some incredible things in this house. Helmer must know the truth. This unhappy secret of Nora's must come out.

KROGSTAD: Very well. If you want to risk it.

MRS. LINDE (*listening again*): Hurry! Go! The dance is over. We aren't safe a moment longer.

KROGSTAD: I'll wait for you downstairs.

MRS. LINDE: Yes, do. You can see me home.

KROGSTAD: I've never been so happy in my life.

(*He goes out through the front door. The door to the hall remains open.*)

MRS. LINDE (*straightening up the room a little and getting ready to leave*): What a change! Oh, what a change! Something to live for! (*Listens*) Ah, here they are. I must get my coat on.

(*She takes her hat and coat.* HELMER's *and* NORA's *voices are heard outside. A key is turned and* HELMER *leads* NORA *almost forcibly into the hall. She is dressed in an Italian costume with a large black shawl. He is in a black cloak.*)

NORA (*still in the doorway, resisting him*): No, no, I want to go back upstairs. I don't want to leave so early.

HELMER: But my dearest Nora—

NORA: Oh, please Torvald. Just another hour!

HELMER: Not another minute, Nora, my sweet. You know what we agreed. Come along, now, into the drawing room. You'll catch cold standing there. (*He leads her into the room, gently but firmly.*)

MRS. LINDE: Good evening.

NORA: Christine!

HELMER: Oh, hello, Mrs. Linde. Are you still here?

MRS. LINDE: Please forgive me. I did so want to see Nora in her costume.

NORA: Have you been sitting here waiting for me?

MRS. LINDE: Yes. I got here too late, I'm afraid. You'd already gone up. And I felt I really shouldn't go back home without seeing you.

HELMER (*taking off* NORA's *shawl*): Well, take a good look at her. Isn't she beautiful, Mrs. Linde?

MRS. LINDE: Oh, yes indeed—

HELMER: Everyone at the party thought so, too. But she's very stubborn . . . the sweet little thing! I nearly had to use force to get her away!

NORA: Oh, Torvald. You'll be sorry you didn't let me stay—even for a half hour longer.

HELMER: You hear that, Mrs. Linde? She dances her tarantella, there's wild applause—which was well deserved. Was I supposed to let her stay after that and spoil the effect? No thank you! I took my lovely little girl, whisked her once around the room—and then the beautiful vision vanished. An exit should always be dramatic, Mrs. Linde. But I can't get Nora to see that. I say, it's hot in here. (*Throws his cloak on a chair and opens the door to his study*) What's this? It's dark in here. Ah, yes—excuse me. (*Goes in and lights some candles*)

NORA (*whispering, breathlessly*): Well?

MRS. LINDE: (*Quietly*) I've spoken to him.

NORA: And . . ?

MRS. LINDE: Nora . . . you must tell your husband everything.

NORA (*disappointed*): I knew it.

MRS. LINDE: You've got nothing to fear from Krogstad. But you must speak to Torvald.

NORA: I won't.

MRS. LINDE: Then the letter will.

NORA: Thank you, Christine. Now I know what I must do. Hush!

HELMER (*entering the room*): Well, Mrs. Linde, have you finished admiring her?

MRS. LINDE: Yes, and now I must say good night.

HELMER: Oh, already?

MRS. LINDE: Yes. Well, good night, Nora, and stop being so stubborn.

HELMER: Well said, Mrs. Linde!

MRS. LINDE: Good night, Mr. Helmer.

HELMER (*accompanying her to the door*): Good night, good night! You'll get home all right, I hope? You haven't far to walk? Good night, good night! (*She exits. He closes the door behind her and returns.*) Well, we've gotten rid of her at last. What a bore that woman is!

Scene 2

The same room. NORA *and* HELMER.

NORA: Aren't you very tired, Torvald?

HELMER: Not in the least. Actually, I feel quite lively. But you look very sleepy.

NORA: Yes, I am. Soon I shall sleep.

HELMER: You see, you see how right I was not to let you stay longer!

NORA: Oh, everything you do is right.

HELMER (*kissing her on the forehead*): That's my little songbird talking common sense. I say, did you notice how cheerful Rank was this evening?

NORA: Oh, was he? I didn't have a chance to speak to him.

HELMER: I hardly did either. But I haven't seen him in such a jolly mood in ages. (*Looks at her for a moment; then comes closer*) Ah, it's wonderful to be back in our own home again and to be all alone with you. You are incredibly beautiful.

NORA: Don't look at me like that, Torvald!

HELMER: What, not look at this wonderful beauty that's mine—all mine?

NORA (*walking around to the other side of the table*): You mustn't talk to me like that tonight.

HELMER (*following her*): You still have the tarantella in your blood, I see. That makes you even more desirable. When I'm out with you among other people as we were tonight, do you know why I say so little to you? Do you know why I stand away from you and only throw you a quick glance? It's because I pretend to myself that you're my secret little sweetheart, and that nobody knows there's anything between us.

NORA: Yes—I know you never think of anything but me.

HELMER: And then when we're about to go, I pretend that you're my young bride. That I'm taking you to my house for the first time—

NORA: Leave me, Torvald! Get away from me!

HELMER: It's just your little game, isn't it, my little Nora?

(*There is a knock on the front door.*)

NORA (*startled*): What was that?

HELMER (*going toward the hall*): Who is it?

RANK: It's me. Can I come in for a minute?

HELMER (*quietly, annoyed*): Oh, what does he want now? (*Calls*) Wait a moment. (*Walks over and opens the door*) Well, nice of you not to go by without looking in.

RANK: I thought I heard your voice, so I felt I had to say good-bye. (*He takes a quick glance around.*) Ah, yes—these dear rooms, how well I know them. What a happy, peaceful home you two have.

HELMER: You seemed to be having a pretty happy time upstairs yourself.

RANK: Why shouldn't I? Why not make the most of things in this world? At least for as long as one can. The wine was excellent.

HELMER: Especially the champagne.

NORA: Torvald drank a lot of champagne this evening. That always makes him merry afterwards.

RANK: Well, why shouldn't a man have a merry evening after a day well spent? (*Slaps him across the back*) That's what I always say, dear fellow.

NORA: Dr. Rank, am I right in thinking you carried out a certain experiment today?

RANK: Exactly.

NORA: And may I congratulate you on the result?

RANK: You may indeed.

NORA: It was good then?

RANK: The best possible finding—for both doctor and patient. Certainty! Absolute certainty. So why shouldn't I have a good time after that?

NORA: Quite right.

HELMER: I agree. As long as you don't suffer for it in the morning.

RANK: Well, you never get anything for nothing in this life.

NORA: Dr. Rank—you like masquerades, don't you?

RANK: Yes, if the disguises are amusing enough.

NORA: Tell me. What shall we two wear at the next masquerade?

HELMER: You silly thing. Are you thinking about the next one already?

RANK: We two? I'll tell you. You must go as Lady Luck . . .

HELMER: How do you find a costume to suggest *that*?

RANK: Your wife only has to wear her everyday clothes—

HELMER: Quite right. Well said! But what are you going to be? Have you decided that?

RANK: Yes, my dear friend. I have decided that.

HELMER: Well?

RANK: At the next masquerade, I shall be invisible.

HELMER: That's a funny idea.

RANK: There's a big, black cloak . . . haven't you heard of the cloak of invisibility? It comes right down over you, and nobody can see you.

HELMER (*trying not to smile*): That's right.

RANK: But I'm forgetting what I came for. Helmer, give me a cigar. One of your black Havanas.

HELMER: With the greatest pleasure. (*Offers him the box*)

RANK (*takes one and cuts off the end*): Thanks.

NORA (*strikes a match*): Let me give you a light.

RANK: Thank you. (*She holds out the match, and he lights his cigar.*) And now—good-bye.

HELMER: Good-bye, good-bye, dear fellow.

NORA: Sleep well, Dr. Rank.

RANK: Thank you for that kind wish.

NORA: Wish me the same.

RANK: You? Very well, since you ask. Sleep well. (*He nods to them both and exits.*)

Scene 3

The same room. NORA *and* HELMER.

HELMER (*quietly*): He's been drinking too much.

(HELMER *takes a bunch of keys from his pocket and goes out into the hall.*)

NORA: Torvald, what do you want out there?

HELMER: I must empty the letter box. It's very full. They'll be no room for the newspapers in the morning. What's this? Someone's been at the lock.

NORA: At the lock?

HELMER: Yes. I'm sure of it. Certainly not one of the maids? Here's a broken hairpin. Nora, it's yours—

NORA (*quickly*): It must have been the children.

HELMER: Well, you'll have to break them of that habit. Ah, that's done it. (*Removes the contents from the box, comes back into the room with the letters in his hand, and shuts the door to the hall*) Look at this! You see how they have piled up. (*Glances through them*) What on earth is this?

NORA (*at the window*): The letter!

HELMER: Two visiting cards—from Dr. Rank.

NORA: From Dr. Rank?

HELMER: Peter Rank, M.D. They were on top. He must have dropped them in as he left.

NORA: Has he written anything on them?

HELMER: There is a black cross above his name. Look. Rather awful, isn't it. It looks as though he was announcing his own death.

NORA: He is.

HELMER: What? Has he told you anything?

NORA: Yes. These cards mean he's said goodbye. He wants to shut himself in his house and die.

HELMER: Poor fellow. I knew I wouldn't be seeing him for much longer. But so soon . . . and hiding himself away like a wounded animal.

NORA: When the time comes, it's best to go silently. Don't you think so, Torvald?

HELMER (*pacing the room*): He was so much a part of our life. I don't think I can imagine him gone. His suffering and loneliness seemed to provide a kind of dark background to the happy sunlight of our marriage. Well, perhaps it's best this way. For him anyway . . . (*stops walking*) and perhaps for us as well. Now there is just the two of us. (*Puts his arms around her*)

NORA (*tearing herself free*): Read your letters now, Torvald.

HELMER: No, not tonight. Tonight I want to be with you, my darling wife—

NORA: When your friend is about to die?

HELMER: You are right. This news has upset both of us. An ugliness has come between us . . . thoughts of death and decay. We must try to forget them. Until then . . . we shall go our separate ways.

NORA (*throwing her arms around his neck*): Good night, Torvald! Good night!

HELMER (*kissing her on the forehead*): Good night, my darling little songbird. Sleep well.

(*He goes into the study and closes the door.*)

NORA (*wild-eyed and pacing around*): Never see him again. Never. (*Throws the shawl over her head*) Never see the children again. Never, never. Oh, that icy black water! Oh,

that bottomless—Oh, if only it were all over!
Now he's reading it. Oh, no, no! Not yet!
Good-bye, Torvald! Good-bye, my darlings.

(She turns to run into the hall. HELMER *throws
open his door and stands there with an open
letter in his hand.)*

HELMER: Nora!

NORA *(crying out)*: Ah!

HELMER: What is this? Do you know what is in
this letter?

NORA: Yes, I know. Let me go! Let me go!

HELMER *(holding her back)*: Go? Where?

NORA *(trying to tear herself loose)*: You mustn't
try to save me, Torvald.

HELMER: Is it true what he writes? How dreadful!

NORA: It is true. I loved you more than anything
else in the whole world.

HELMER: Oh, don't try to make silly excuses.

NORA *(taking a step toward him)*: Torvald—

HELMER: Miserable woman—what have you done?

NORA: Let me go! You're not going to suffer for
my sake. I won't let you!

HELMER: Stop play-acting. *(Locks the front door)*
You are going to stay here and explain
yourself. Do you understand what you've
done? Answer me. Do you understand?

NORA *(her face hardening)*: Yes, now I am
beginning to understand.

HELMER (*walking around the room*): Oh, what a terrible awakening this is! For eight years . . . this woman who was my pride and joy . . . a liar, worse than that, a criminal! (NORA *remains silent and looks straight at him.*) I should have guessed something like this would happen. I should have seen it coming. All your father's irresponsible ways are coming out in you. Oh, this is my punishment for turning a blind eye to him. I did it for your sake, and now you reward me like this.

NORA: Yes. Like this.

HELMER: Now you have destroyed all my happiness. You have ruined my whole future. I'm done for, a miserable failure. And it's all the fault of a feather-brained woman!

NORA: When I'm gone from this world, you will be free.

HELMER: Oh, stop pretending. What good would it do me if you left this world behind, as you put it? Not the slightest bit of good. He could still let it all come out, if he likes. And if he does, people might even suspect me as an accomplice in these crimes. Now do you understand what you have done to me?

NORA (*coldly and calmly*): Yes.

HELMER: We must see about putting things right. I must try to buy him off somehow. This thing must be hushed up at any price. As far as you and I are concerned, things must appear to go on exactly as before. But only in the eyes of the world, of course. You'll go on living here, that's understood. But you will not be allowed to bring up the children. I can't trust you with them. (*The doorbell rings.* HELMER *gives a start.*) What's that? So late? Hide yourself, Nora. Say you're ill.

(NORA *does not move.* HELMER *goes to the door and opens it.*)

MAID: A letter for madam.

HELMER: Give it to me. (*Grabs the letter and shuts the door*) It's from him. You can't have it. I want to read it myself.

NORA: Read it.

HELMER: I hardly dare. This may mean the end for both of us. No, I must know. (*He opens the note quickly, reads a few lines, and cries out in joy.*) Nora! Nora! I must read it again. Yes, it's true! I am saved! Nora, I am saved!

NORA: What about me?

HELMER: You, too, of course. We are both saved. Look, he's sent your IOU back. He writes that he's sorry for what has happened. His luck has changed. Oh, Nora, Nora—no, first let me destroy this filthy thing. (*He tears up the IOU and both letters, throws all the pieces into the stove, and watches them burn.*) Well, that's the end of that. He wrote that you have known since Christmas Eve. You must have had three horrible days of it.

NORA: Yes. It's been a hard fight.

HELMER: Well, it's all over. Why this grim look on your face? Oh, of course, I understand. You can't believe that I have forgiven you. But I have, Nora, I swear. I know you did it because you loved me.

NORA: That is true.

HELMER: You have loved me as a wife should love her husband. It was simply because of your innocence that you chose the wrong means. You mustn't mind the hard words I said to you in those first dreadful moments. My whole world seemed to be tumbling down around my ears. I have forgiven you, Nora. I swear.

NORA: Thank you for your forgiveness.

(*She goes out through the door, right.*)

HELMER: No, don't go—(*looks in*). What are you doing?

NORA (*offstage*): Taking off this fancy dress.

HELMER (*standing at the open door*): Yes, do. Try to get some rest, and set your mind at peace again. You know you are safe and sound under my wing. (*Walks up and down near the door*) How lovely and peaceful this little home of ours is. Here you can find safety. Never be frightened of anything again, Nora. Just open your heart to me. I'll make all the decisions for you . . . What's this? You've changed your clothes?

NORA (*in her everyday dress*): Yes, Torvald. I've changed.

HELMER: But why now—so late?

NORA: I shall not sleep tonight. (*Looks at her watch*) It isn't that late. Sit down here, Torvald. You and I have a lot to talk about.

(*She sits down at one end of the table.*)

HELMER (*sitting down on the other side of the table*): You frighten me. I don't understand you.

NORA: No, that's just it. You don't understand me. And I've never understood you—until this evening.

HELMER: What do you mean?

NORA: We have been married for eight years. Has it occurred to you that this is the first time that we've had a serious talk?

HELMER: Serious? What do you mean, serious?

NORA: In eight whole years, we have never exchanged a serious word on a serious subject.

HELMER: What did you want me to do? Drag you into all my worries that you couldn't possibly have helped me with?

NORA: I'm not talking about worries. I'm simply saying that we have never sat down and tried to get to the bottom of anything.

HELMER: But what on earth has that got to do with you?

NORA: That's just the point. You have never understood me. I've been greatly wronged, Torvald, first by my father and then by you.

HELMER: What? But we two have loved you more than anything in the world!

NORA (*shaking her head*): You have never loved me. You thought it was fun to be in love with me.

HELMER: Nora, what kind of a way is this to talk?

NORA: It's the truth, Torvald. When I lived with Father, he used to tell me what he thought about everything. I never had any opinions but his. And if I did have any of my own, I kept them quiet because he wouldn't have liked them. He called me his little doll. Then I came to live in your house—

HELMER: What kind of a way is that to describe our marriage?

NORA: I passed out of Father's hands into yours. You arranged everything the way you wanted it, so I simply took over your taste in everything. Or I pretended to. I don't know. You and Father did me a great wrong. It's your fault that I have done nothing with my life.

HELMER: Nora, how ungrateful you are. Haven't you been happy here?

NORA: No, never. I used to think I was. But I haven't ever been happy.

HELMER: Not—not happy?

NORA: No. I have been your doll-wife, just as at home I was Father's doll-child. That's all our marriage has been, Torvald.

HELMER: There may be some truth in what you say, though you exaggerate it. But from now on it will be different. Playtime is over. Now the time has come for education.

NORA: Oh, Torvald, you are not the man to teach me how to be the right wife for you. I must take steps to educate myself, and you can't help me with that. It's something I must do on my own. That's why I'm leaving you.

HELMER (*jumping up*): What did you say?

NORA: I'm leaving you at once. Christine will put me up for the night—

HELMER: You can't do this! I forbid you!

NORA: It's no use to forbid anything now. I shall take with me nothing but what is mine. I don't want anything from you, now or ever.

HELMER: But to leave your home, your husband and children! Don't you care what people will say?

NORA: I can't help that. I only know that I must do this.

HELMER: First and foremost you are a wife and mother.

NORA: I don't believe that any longer. I believe that first and foremost I am a human being—like you. Or at least I must try to become one. I know most people agree with you, Torvald, and that's what it says in books. But I'm no longer prepared to accept what people say and what's written in books. I must think things out for myself and try to find my own answers.

HELMER: Don't you have any moral feelings left?

NORA: Oh, Torvald, that isn't an easy question to answer. I simply don't know. I'm very confused about such things. I've also learned that the law is different from what I thought. Has a woman really no right to spare her dying father pain or to save her husband's life? I don't believe that.

HELMER: You're talking like a child. You don't understand how society works.

NORA: No, I don't. But I intend to learn. I must try to discover who is right, society or me.

HELMER: I almost believe that you are out of your mind.

NORA: I've never felt so sane and sure.

HELMER: Then there is only one possible explanation. You don't love me any more.

NORA: Yes, that's exactly it.

HELMER: Nora! How can you say this to me?

NORA: I'm very sorry to have to say it, Torvald. You have always been so kind to me. But I can't help it. I don't love you any longer.

HELMER: Can you explain why I have lost your love?

NORA: Yes, I can. It happened this evening when the miracle failed to happen. It was then that I realized that you weren't the man I thought you were.

HELMER: I don't understand you.

NORA: For eight years, I have waited patiently. I don't believe that miracles happen every day. Then this awful business happened to me and I thought: "Now this miracle will take place!" When Krogstad's letter was lying out there, it never occurred to me for a moment that you would let that man triumph over you. I *knew* you would say to him: "Tell the whole world if you like."

HELMER: Then what?

NORA: Then I was certain that you'd step forward and take the blame yourself.

HELMER: Nora!

NORA: But would I have accepted such a sacrifice from you? No, of course I wouldn't. That was the miracle I was both hoping for and dreading. To stop it, I was ready to end my life.

HELMER: Nora, I would gladly work day and night for you. But no man sacrifices his honor, even for the person he loves.

NORA: Millions of women have done it.

HELMER: You think and talk like a stupid child.

NORA: That may be. But you neither think nor talk like the man I could share my life with. Once the danger was past, you acted like nothing had happened. I was your little songbird again, your little doll, exactly like before. Except you would have to protect it twice as much as before, now that it had shown itself to be so weak. (*Gets up*) That was the moment I realized that for eight years I was living with a stranger . . . that I had born him three children. Oh, I can't bear to think of it.

HELMER (*sadly*): I see. There is a great gulf dividing us. But Nora, is there some way we might bridge it? I still have it in me to change.

NORA: Perhaps . . . if your doll goes away.

HELMER: I can't be separated from you! No, no, Nora. I can't even think of that happening.

NORA (*going into the room, right*): All the more reason why it should be done.

(*She comes back wearing her coat and carrying a small traveling bag.*)

NORA: Good-bye, Torvald. I don't want to see the children. I know they're in better hands than mine. As I am now, I can be nothing to them.

HELMER: But some day, Nora, some day—

NORA: How can I tell? I've no idea what will happen to me.

HELMER: Nora, will you never think of me?

NORA: Yes, of course. I will think of you and the children and this house.

HELMER: Can't I help you if you ever need it?

NORA: I don't accept things from strangers.

HELMER: Can I ever be anything more to you than a stranger?

NORA: Only by a miracle of miracles. You and I would have to change so much that—oh, Torvald, I don't believe in miracles any more.

HELMER: But I want to believe in them. Tell me. Change so much so that—?

NORA: That our life together could become a marriage. Good-bye. (*She goes out through the hall door.*)

HELMER (*sinking down on a chair*): Nora! Nora! (*Looks around and gets up*) Empty! She's gone! (*A hope strikes him.*) But wait . . . the miracle of miracles—?

(*The street door is slammed shut downstairs. Curtain*)